COINS
COVENANT
& Character

ISBN: 978-1-59684-675-3
Copyright © 2012 by "Kindle the Power" series—a Discipleship Emphasis for International Women's Discipleship.
All Rights Reserved
Printed in the United States of America

Foreword

Coins, Covenant & Character is part of International Women's Discipleship *Kindle the Power* discipleship resources.

Kindle the Power from International Women's Discipleship, was initiated from a heartfelt desire to provide quality Pentecostal Bible studies as well as an avenue for Christian growth for our discipleship emphasis. *Kindle the Power* focuses on the acrostic POWER:

P Prayer and Praise (*eucharisteo* — giving thanks — Phil. 4:11-12)

O Others (reaching into our communities; blessing through missions)

W Word of God (Enliven Inductive Bible Study)

E Effecting change in our lives and the lives of others (through spiritual accountability and covenant)

R Relationships (Friendship Evangelism) Repentance

Kindle the Power encourages women to journal their *power* walk so they can reflect on past victories and insights, find direction in their current circumstances, and be a lifelong testimony and legacy of the grace of God for generations to come. You can order your journal(s) from International Women's Discipleship or Pathway Press.

Rhonda K. Holland, a personal friend and mentor, is author of *Coins, Covenant & Character*, the second study in Rhonda's series. The first in her Bible study series was *Giants, Grapes & Grasshoppers.* The next study in Rhonda's series is *Pots, Pans & Prophecies,* which will be available in the early part of 2013. Throughout these studies you will find Rhonda's teaching to be inspiring, refreshing, and encouraging. Through God's anointing, Rhonda challenges us to take a look at our "coins of covenant" through the eyes of the Great Physician. We are challenged to take a closer look at how these coins are played out in our lives. Her anointed teaching through DVD and Bible study will take you on a journey of seeing yourself through the eyes of our Great Physician. You will walk through the recovery room as you find the coins you have lost and are restored.

In any project like this there are many people who give of their time and talents. I want to express special appreciation to our author, Rhonda K. Holland, for her dedication to minister through the written word; for her believing in my vision for providing quality Pentecostal Bible studies; and for allowing me to "stretch" her into new areas of ministry with our teaching DVDs; creative thanks to Annette Alsobrooks at Ballew Graphics for the cover, and graphic design of *Coins, Covenant & Character;* special thanks to Chad Guyton and the 5:01 Studios team for their professional work on the DVD; Pathway Press, Terry Hart (director) and David Ray (marketing) for partnering with us on our *Kindle the Power* projects and for believing in our passion for discipleship resources; Michael McDonald for

his help on flow editing our project; my husband, David, for his love and patience during this process; Lenae Simmons, assistant to my husband, for always lending a helping hand when needed; and a very special thanks to my assistant, Pamela Kay Overbey, for her diligence in helping to edit this project from beginning to end.

My prayer is that we will all be able to say, "Rejoice with me, I have found my lost coin."

—Lorna V. Gosnell
International Women's Discipleship Coordinator

Introduction

Coins, Covenant & Character

COINS, COVENANT & CHARACTER

by Rhonda K. Holland

Introduction

Women really enjoy spiritual retreats! I am no exception. I appreciate the opportunity retreats provide to fellowship with Christian women of all walks of life, various backgrounds and ages. It does not matter where we come from or where we have been, our common faith makes us bond. Lasting friendships are often formed or strengthened at these events.

The fall of the year seems to be a favorite time to schedule these retreats. My personal schedule is very busy during this time of the year, and I love it! The fall of 2011 was no exception. I had numerous retreats and conferences scheduled. I was looking forward to each one with excitement and anticipation.

It was during this busy season that this Bible study, *Coins, Covenant & Character*, was birthed. I was preparing for a retreat that began on September 30, 2011, with a wonderful group of ladies that I have been privileged to speak for each year for some time now. Before going to bed the night before, I prayed and asked God to bless the retreat and every lady attending. I asked for direction and for Him to bless the messages I had prepared for the weekend. I was excited because I have grown fond of these ladies over the years and really looked forward to their

fellowship. God never fails to show up and minister to us. And the fact that the retreat was going to be held at the beautiful Folly Beach in Charleston, South Carolina, only added to the excitement.

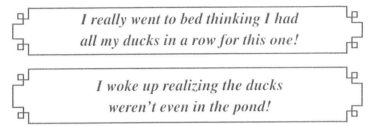

I really went to bed thinking I had all my ducks in a row for this one!

I woke up realizing the ducks weren't even in the pond!

Just before waking up the next morning, I had a very real and unusual dream. In the dream, I saw nothing. I simply heard a voice. I heard this statement and nothing else: *"Consider the woman who lost the coin, for there is much there."* I woke up knowing I had to follow through with this command. My mind immediately went to the woman Jesus spoke of in Luke 15:8-9:

> Or suppose a woman has ten silver coins and loses one. Does she not light a lamp, sweep the house and search carefully until she finds it? And when she finds it, she calls her friends and neighbors together and says, "Rejoice with me; I have found my lost coin" (NIV 1984).

Nothing went as I had planned. The day got off to a very hectic start and continued on right up until I left for the retreat. I had no time to stop and research or study the topic of the "woman who lost the coin." As I was driving to the retreat, I was praying and "explaining" my situation to God. I assured Him

INTRODUCTION

that I had heard the instruction to look into this and I would as soon as I completed this retreat. But I continued to feel that familiar stirring in my heart. I knew the Lord wanted this topic for this retreat! My conversation continued with the Lord, "But God, I am already on I-26 nearing Charleston! (*As if He didn't know!*) How can I possibly understand what You are wanting me to see about this woman in time to teach it for this group of ladies *tonight?*"

I couldn't shake the feeling that I needed to do something about the dream and what the Lord had shown me. Traveling alone, I couldn't research the project and drive. I pulled over and called my sister who lives in Mississippi. I explained my dilemma to her. "Jana, help me! Please stop what you are doing, get online and do a search on the commentary that goes with the phrase 'the woman who lost the coin.' I need for you to read to me while I drive." I put her on speakerphone and continued my drive to Charleston. She began reading to me what she was finding in the commentary. The more she read, the more I felt confirmation from God that I was to teach on this particular topic at the retreat. She discovered a wealth of information from various commentaries and historians. In summation, this is what I heard:

> *When a Jewish woman was chosen to become a bride, she was given a bridal headpiece consisting of ten coins by her father. She didn't earn the coins. They were a symbolic gift. When she accepted this headpiece, she was making an oath that she would walk in covenant with the bridegroom and his family.*

The coins were worn in the same way we may wear an engagement ring or wedding band today. The coins could never be taken away from her by a creditor, even if she owed him money she couldn't pay. They were respected as representation of her covenant by all who saw them. If she removed one and used it for purchases it was considered disrespectful to her husband, and she wasn't allowed to do this without his permission. If she willfully walked out of her covenant with her husband, he may actually remove a coin as a symbol of her unfaithfulness for all to see! So, these coins were valued much more than their actual worth because they represented her covenant and her faithfulness to that covenant.

No wonder the woman Jesus referred to in the parable became very proactive in finding her lost coin!

Remember in my dream I was told to "consider the woman who lost the coin," not the parable of the lost coin. The more my sister read to me, the more my heart began to feel the presence of God as I considered this woman and the significance she clearly understood concerning the value of her lost coin. Perhaps when Jesus shared this parable, there was a woman standing there who had experienced the pain of losing a covenant coin. Maybe she had known the shame of

"Consider the woman who lost the coin"

having a coin taken from her. I believe when Jesus was speaking this parable, He was very likely looking into the face of a woman who felt and understood His meaning.

As Jana continued to read, I immediately felt compelled to have her turn to Colossians 3 and read the chapter to me. This passage deals in detail about the character of Christ that we are to make a part of our lives as we enter into covenant with Him. When we accept the free gift of salvation, we receive a robe of righteousness by our Father signifying that we have entered into covenant with the Bridegroom Jesus. As the woman who received the bridal headpiece bearing ten coins did not earn those coins, neither do we earn our salvation. However, we do enter into a commitment to live a life of character pleasing to Christ. These characteristics of our new redeemed nature are given in Colossians 3. And there are ten character traits that we must have as a believer outlined in this chapter! These ten traits will become our "ten coins of covenant" throughout this study.

In a short drive on I-26 near Charleston, the Lord birthed a series of messages in my heart for that retreat and for the next several retreats that were scheduled. These messages, as I heeded the instruction to "consider the woman who lost the coin," have made a tremendous impact on my life and I feel compelled to share them.

In this series of lessons, it is so important that you take the time to journal and ponder deeply your walk and covenant with God. He is calling us to a life of real commitment with Him, especially as we see the day of His glorious return quickly approaching.

Like the Jewish bride and her commitment to the bridegroom and his family, when we become part of the body of Christ, we make a commitment to Jesus to live a life fulfilling our covenant and to walk according to the nature of Christ before other believers and the world. The character of Christ reflected in us is a constant witness to the believer and nonbeliever alike. We will discuss the importance of that commitment and why it is necessary to live a life of character, especially in these last days, as a testimony of our covenant to the Lord.

Let's purpose together over the next six weeks to learn how to keep our coins of covenant and find those we may have lost. It is my prayer that when we finish this Bible study, like the woman in the parable Jesus shared, we will be rejoicing together over having all our coins of covenant intact and the character of Christ will be evident every day in us and through us.

Week One

POWER TRUTH

Week One
POWER TRUTH
Consider the Woman

Take time to consider your covenant with Christ. Ask God to reveal to you areas of both personal strengths and weaknesses. As we focus on the restoration and recovery of our lost coins in this study, purpose in your heart to find what you may have lost or neglected in your commitment to Christ.

Focus on these scriptures as you read and journal this week:

> Search me [thoroughly], O God, and know my heart! Try me and know my thoughts! And see if there is any wicked or hurtful way in me, and lead me in the way everlasting (Ps. 139:23-24 AB).

> Stand fast therefore in the liberty by which Christ has made us free, and do not be entangled again with a yoke of bondage (Gal. 5:1).

Week One

Study: Consider the Woman

Week One
CONSIDER THE WOMAN
Luke 15:8-10

Or suppose a woman has ten silver coins and loses one. Does she not light a lamp, sweep the house and search carefully until she finds it? And when she finds it, she calls her friends and neighbors together and says, "Rejoice with me; I have found my lost coin" (Luke 15:8-9 NIV 1984).

Let's look again at the information we discussed in our introduction:

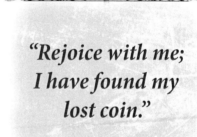

When a Jewish woman was chosen to become a bride, she was given a bridal headpiece consisting of ten coins by her father. She

> **"Rejoice with me; I have found my lost coin."**

didn't earn the coins. They were a symbolic gift. When she accepted this headpiece, she was making an oath that she would walk in covenant with the bridegroom and his family. The coins were worn in the same way we may wear an engagement ring or wedding band today. The coins could never be taken away from her by a creditor, even if she owed him

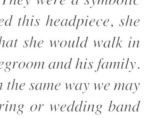

money she couldn't pay. They were respected as representation of her covenant by all who saw them. If she removed one and used it for purchases it was considered disrespectful to her husband, and she wasn't allowed to do this without his permission. If she willfully walked out of her covenant with her husband, he may actually remove a coin as a symbol of her unfaithfulness for all to see.

These coins were valued much more than their actual worth because they represented her covenant and her faithfulness to that covenant.

I have often thought of this passage of Scripture and the excitement that finding the lost coin created. This woman, when she recovered what she had lost, called her friends and neighbors together to celebrate. We know from historical accounts, that when the Jewish people celebrated with family and friends, often there was a great feast and a party atmosphere to enhance the rejoicing. Obviously, the celebration alone would cost more than the worth of the coin. That thought further enhances the probability that the value of the coin was based on what it represented, rather than its actual worth.

Jesus was a powerful teacher and illustrated His points in ways that were clearly understood to those who really listened. I imagine when He spoke these powerful parables in Luke 15, He spoke to those present with illustrations that applied to their everyday lives and work. This chapter begins by telling us that all the tax collectors and the sinners drew near to hear Him. What a group had gathered around Jesus! But the love He had for them was so real that they were drawn to Him. He spoke to them with words and references they understood.

> ### *Take the time as you study this week to read Luke 15.*

The powerful parables Jesus shared in Luke 15 teach us so much about the love of God for the lost and His desire to compel them to come home. This chapter also serves to remind the self-righteous Pharisees of God's grace, restoration and forgiveness extended to the sinner. This passage delivered a message of compassion for the lost, comfort for the saved, and conviction for the judgmental Pharisees.

We have all experienced church services when the preached or taught Word brought comfort to the believer and conviction to the sinner all at the same time. The Word is so powerful and often contains multiple, layered messages in its passages without altering the clear truth presented in the printed verses. While the parables in this chapter are a very clear revelation of the love Jesus has for the lost, I am certain they also ministered to those standing in the crowd that day as His words reached out to the individuals present.

The Word of God is amazing. It is inexhaustible. It is alive with the power of God. It speaks to us in so many ways.

> For the Word that God speaks is alive and full of power [making it active, operative, energizing, and effective]; it is sharper than any two-edged sword, penetrating to the

dividing line of the breath of life (soul) and [the immortal] spirit, and of joints and marrow [of the deepest parts of our nature], exposing and sifting and analyzing and judging the very thoughts and purposes of the heart (Heb. 4:12 AB).

> *Take a moment and write a passage of Scripture that has come alive in your heart during a time of crisis in your life.*

_____

_____

_____

_____

_____

_____

_____

_____

_____

_____

> *What is it about the passage you have chosen that brings you comfort?*

_____

_____

_____

_____

_____

_____

_____

_____

_____

In the first portion of this chapter in Luke, Jesus shared the parable of the lost sheep. Let's imagine the group that had assembled to hear Jesus. In my mind, I can see a group of shepherds standing near. These men clearly understood the importance of retrieving the sheep that had strayed away from the safety of the fold. They probably spoke to each other about the times they had been like that shepherd Jesus spoke about. Many times they had left their own flock to go out in the darkness and bring in the one little lost and helpless lamb. Can you imagine the revelation they had as they saw the Lord as their Shepherd, lovingly seeking for them to bring them out of danger? They understood what He was saying because they had experienced it! And now they could feel the compassion of the Shepherd as they listened to Him speak.

In the third parable of this passage, Jesus shared the beloved story of the prodigal son and the grief of the father. It was the same father's love that caused the son to return to his home. Quite possibly there was a father in the crowd who immediately pulled in closer to Jesus as He began this parable. I envision this man in the crowd who was experiencing the hurt of betrayal from his own son. Perhaps his beloved son was still away enjoying his freedom while his father grieved not knowing what dangers may befall him. As Jesus spoke, this dad became hopeful and was encouraged that his love, the strong love of a faithful father, would draw his wayward son home again. Yes, this man would have understood what Jesus meant! He felt the connection with the parable on a very real and personal level. Did the heavenly

Father grieve and desire fellowship with him the way he did for his lost son? Something about this parable made this dad want to run to his heavenly Father. He wanted restoration with Him! And his love for his son would draw him home! The way Jesus told the story gave this father hope that his story would end well also.

> **And right in the middle of these parables, Jesus told us to consider the woman who lost a coin.**

I visualize a warm, summer day. A woman was standing with hot sand under her feet and a crowd was gathered. People were pressing in to hear the words of this man called Jesus that everyone was talking about. Some said that when He spoke it was as if He looked right into your very soul, knew your thoughts, and heard your heart's cry. Many were comforted and drawn to Him because of His insight, and others wanted to run away from Him because of it.

Consider the woman!

As this Jewish woman moved in closer, she understood what the others meant when they had spoken of this Jesus. She was drawn to His compassion and gentle love. His words of wisdom wrapped her heart in comfort. She had heard testimonies of those who had been changed by Him. Their brokenness had been mended and their hope

restored. And yet while she hungered to be free from her own failures, she was also fearful He would see and expose her sins and struggles. But even more than her fear of exposure and shame, she desired acceptance and understanding, even forgiveness from this Teacher, Prophet, Man, she did not know. What was it about Him that made her want to be near Him and understand His words and His teaching? What was this pull in her heart to Him that made her lay down her fear of rejection in hopes He would speak to her heart and comfort her? She pressed in, hoping to see Him, but not certain if she wanted to be seen by Him. And then it happened. He looked directly at her. He looked into her very heart and said, "Or suppose a woman has ten silver coins and loses one." Her heart pounded! Did He know about her failures? Did He know that she had reason to have lost a coin? Did He know that she was troubled and considered breaking her covenant? And He continued . . . "Does she not light a lamp, sweep the house and search carefully until she finds it?" Was He trying to tell her that it would be all right? Was He trying to make her understand that what she had lost in her relationship with her husband could be restored? Was He wanting her to realize that her situation really wasn't hopeless? Did He want her to stop and consider the value of her covenant and know that all that was lost really could be found? As if He was hearing her heart's cry, He added, "And when she finds it, she calls her friends and neighbors together and says, 'Rejoice with me; I have found my lost coin.'" He smiled at her and her heart was so moved by this unspoken revelation.

He understood! He knew her warfare! He knew her struggles! But He had given her hope! Hope that all that had been taken and lost could be—yes would be—restored.

> *Restoration of what has been lost—that is what this study is about.*

> *Like the woman in this passage, we will find our lost "coin" and gain back all it represents.*

In this study, we will be asking God to search our hearts and see if there is anything about our character that He desires to change. We will read the Word concerning what our character should be as a believer and how it contradicts our old sinful nature. It is so important that you yield your heart to hear Him and purpose to allow the Holy Spirit to have His way in every area of your life as we go forward in this study.

> *Read this passage and in your own words make it into a personal prayer:*

Search me [thoroughly], O God, and know my heart! Try me and know my thoughts! And see if there is any wicked or hurtful way in me, and lead me in the way everlasting (Ps. 139:23-24 AB).

_____

_____

_____

_____

_____

_____

Let's look at some familiar scripture that makes us aware of what we gained when we entered into covenant with Christ:

> And you He made alive, who were dead in trespasses and sins, in which you once walked according to the course of this world, according to the prince of the power of the air, the spirit who now works in the sons of disobedience, among whom also we all once conducted ourselves in the lusts of our flesh, fulfilling the desires of the flesh and of the mind, and were by nature children of wrath, just as the others. But God, who is rich in mercy, because of His great love with which He loved us, even when we were dead in trespasses, made us alive together with Christ (by grace you have been saved), and raised us up together, and made us sit together in the heavenly places in Christ Jesus, that in the ages to come He might show the exceeding riches of His grace in His kindness toward us in Christ Jesus. For by grace you have been saved through faith, and that not of yourselves; it is the gift of God, not of works, lest anyone should boast. For we are His workmanship, created in Christ Jesus for good works, which God prepared beforehand that we should walk in them (Eph. 2:1-10).

What a wonderful and comforting passage of Scripture! It reminds us that our God is rich in mercy and His love toward us is great. He loved us even when we were dead in the trespasses of our sins! His glorious and amazing grace has saved us and now we are raised up together. We are made to sit in heavenly places in Christ! The scripture declares that we are saved by grace, through faith. When we accept Christ as our Savior, the Holy Spirit imparts new life and we experience the wonderful miracle of the new birth. We are born into the family of God! We enter into covenant with Him! Once we become a part of the body of Christ all things become new.

But there is a very real and ongoing conflict between our flesh nature and our spirit. To be victorious, we are instructed to crucify our flesh and walk in the spirit.

> ***Read Galatians 5 in your study time this week.***
> ***Meditate on verses 24 and 25:***

And those who are Christ's have crucified the flesh with its passions and desires. If we live in the Spirit, let us also walk in the Spirit (vv. 24-25).

As believers, we desire to live a life pleasing to Christ. We know what it is to walk in sweet fellowship with the Lord. We have known the joy of overcoming temptations and winning the battles of the spiritual warfare around us. But we are also aware of the Enemy's desire to cause us to lose what God has given us. Satan wants to take away our Christian character and rob us of our new nature that we were given when we were redeemed. He does not want us to walk in covenant with Christ because he knows

the power that a Christian experiences as a result of a dedicated commitment and a constant walk in the Spirit. Satan desires for our flesh to rise up and our old nature to once again dominate us. The devil, our Enemy, comes to steal, kill and destroy what God desires for us to have in our covenant relationship with Him.

> The thief does not come except to steal, and to kill, and to destroy. I have come that they may have life, and that they may have it more abundantly (John 10:10).

In the same verse that describes the intention of the Enemy, we see that Jesus came that we might have abundant life. Jesus wants to restore back to us what the Enemy has stolen or has caused us to lose in our battles in this life.

Take a moment and think of the joy you experienced when you became a Christian. The amazing feeling of victory and peace that overwhelmed you when you experienced salvation was and is indescribable! It felt as if the weight of the world had been lifted off your shoulders! But, as we continue our journey as a follower of Christ, we begin to understand spiritual warfare. The Enemy desires to put us off the path of righteousness and bind us in discouragement, stealing our freedom and joy. He wants to rob us of our peace and take away our new nature and put us in bondage again to the things of the flesh. We must purpose daily to walk in covenant with God, allowing our new nature to be strengthened.

I have been crucified with Christ; it is no longer I who live, but Christ lives in me; and the life which I now live in the flesh I live by faith in the Son of God, who loved me and gave Himself for me (Gal. 2:20).

> ***Write in your own words what you believe this verse means and instructs us to do.***

_____

_____

_____

_____

_____

_____

_____

_____

_____

_____

_____

Remember, the purpose of this study is for us to find what we have lost. Together, we will consider the woman who has felt so much pain at the hands of others that she has lost her desire to forgive. We will consider the woman who has known so much rejection that she has lost her compassion. We will consider the woman who feels so much of the pressures of her responsibilities that she has lost her joy in serving others.

But now consider the woman *you* know best. What have you lost that you hope to regain? Have you found it difficult in recent trials to walk in your new

nature and have the character of Christ? Have you lost a coin of covenant and found your old nature resurfacing in times of stress?

Remember, the Enemy does not want us to walk in covenant with Christ because he knows the power that comes with a dedicated commitment and a constant walk in the Spirit.

As you journal this week, ask God to help you to walk according to Galatians 5.

Memorize Galatians 5:1:

Stand fast therefore in the liberty by which Christ has made us free, and do not be entangled again with a yoke of bondage.

Read Colossians 3:1-17 in preparation for next week's lesson and look at the contrast between the carnality of the flesh and the character of the believer in this passage.

Consider the woman *you* know best!

Week Two

POWER TRUTH

Week Two
POWER TRUTH
Counting My Coins

Read Colossians 3 this week and focus on the Ccharacter of the believer. We are to walk in our redeemed and new nature as a follower of Jesus. Take time to familiarize yourself with the list of characteristics that are to be demonstrated in our daily walk:

Compassion

Kindness

Humility

Meekness

Longsuffering

Forbearance

Forgiveness

Love

Peace

Gratitude

With renewed determination, purpose every day of your life and especially when faced with difficulties to respond as the Spirit of God leads you, always demonstrating these characteristics.

Hold tightly to your coins of covenant!

Week Two

Study: Counting My Coins

Week Two
COUNTING MY COINS
Colossians 3:12-15

I shared with you in the introduction of this study how I felt compelled to have my sister turn to Colossians 3 and read that chapter to me as I drove to the retreat in Charleston. This passage deals in detail about the character of Christ that we are to make a part of our lives as we walk in covenant with Him. When we accept the free gift of salvation, we receive a robe of righteousness by our Father signifying that we have entered into covenant with the Bridegroom Jesus Christ. As the woman who received the bridal headpiece bearing ten coins did not earn those coins, neither do we earn our salvation. However, we do make a commitment to live a life of character pleasing to Christ. No, we do not work our way to Heaven or earn our salvation by good deeds, but we are called to walk in obedience to His Word.

Think about this verse:

> The wages of sin is death, but the gift of God is eternal life in Christ Jesus our Lord (Rom. 6:23).

There are two words in this verse that we need to think about: wages and gift. Wages are earned. A gift is given. Those who continually *refuse* the gift of salvation, who *tread* on His grace, who *deny* their

COINS, COVENANT& CHARACTER *39*

own access to His tender mercy, who *trample* under foot daily His offer of forgiveness, actually "earn" their way to eternal damnation. They *rebel* against the gentle wooing of the Holy Spirit and *neglect* so great a salvation. The wages of sin is death. So, we are reminded through this verse of two very important truths: the unrepentant sinner chooses to earn the wages that purchase eternal death, but salvation through Jesus Christ is a gift offered to all who will receive it. I am persuaded that those who stand before God in judgment, having refused the gift of salvation, will realize that they earned their passage to hell. What a sad revelation. But the redeemed will rejoice with a heart of love and gratitude, knowing His mercy and great amazing grace gave access to eternal life.

We are the blessed recipients of His wonderful gift of salvation when we accept Jesus as our Savior, and eternal life is a gift from God. We receive our redeemed nature and all things become new. And we are instructed to "put off the old" (Col. 3: 9) and "put on the new" (v. 10). We are called to a life of obedience to our covenant with Christ.

> Do not lie to one another, since you have put off the old man with his deeds, and have put on the new man who is renewed in knowledge according to the image of Him who created him (vv. 9-10).

The flesh nature is to be put to death and the new nature is to come alive. The characteristics of our new redeemed nature are given in the following verses of

the same chapter. Read verses 12 to 15. There are ten character traits that we must have as a believer given in these verses. *These ten traits will become our ten coins of covenant throughout this study.*

Let's take a closer look at this passage together:

> Therefore, as the elect of God, holy and beloved, put on tender mercies, kindness, humility, meekness, longsuffering; bearing with one another, and forgiving one another, if anyone has a complaint against another; even as Christ forgave you, so you also must do. But above all these things put on love, which is the bond of perfection. And let the peace of God rule in your hearts, to which also you were called in one body; and be thankful (vv. 12-15).

From these verses, let's look at the ten characteristics listed that are so important in our lives:

- Compassion (tender mercies) (v. 12)
- Kindness
- Humility
- Meekness
- Longsuffering
- Forbearance (bearing with one another) (v. 13)
- Forgiveness (forgiving one another)
- Love (v. 14)
- Peace (v. 15)
- Gratitude (be thankful)

Write a prayer from your heart asking God to increase all of these coins of covenant in your daily walk. Ask Him for strength to display these characteristics in your life, especially in times of spiritual warfare.

_____

_____

_____

_____

_____

_____

_____

_____

_____

_____

We have all faced situations that made us feel that we were lacking in some of these characteristics. We have also experienced His presence and His strength and allowed Christlike actions to show forth in our response in a painful place in our Christian journey. We all want to please Jesus and walk in consistency with Him. But there are those days that it can seem more difficult to do so.

> We have all experienced His presence and His strength . . .

Have you lost your coin of compassion with that person that is constantly causing you pain? Perhaps

you recently found it difficult to display your coin of kindness because everyone else around you seems to be harsh and negative. Maybe you feel you haven't shown the coin of longsuffering in the darkness of your valley. Have you kept your coin of forgiveness intact by forgiving those who seem to continually hurt you? Perhaps you have lost your coin of gratitude for the good things in your life because the Enemy has caused you to focus on what seems to be wrong in your world.

These thoughts are not suggested to make you feel condemnation, but rather to help you get back what you may have lost. We all have times when we are stronger in times of trials and then there are those times when we feel like we "lose it" in our attitude. It is in those times that we react instead of respond to a situation.

> *Look over the list of our coins of covenant. Be honest with yourself as you journal this week. Prayerfully take the time to consider the coins   you feel you are more apt to "lose" in your times of crisis.*

It is also so important for us to remember that with every "missing coin" we give an opportunity to the Enemy to gain ground in our lives. He has access to us through our old nature.

Ephesians 4:20-32 confirms this. Let's read together:

> But you have not so learned Christ, if indeed you have heard Him and have been taught by Him, as the truth is in Jesus: that you put

off, concerning your former conduct, the old man which grows corrupt according to the deceitful lusts, and be renewed in the spirit of your mind, and that you put on the new man which was created according to God, in true righteousness and holiness. Therefore, putting away lying, "Let each one of you speak truth with his neighbor," for we are members of one another. "Be angry, and do not sin": do not let the sun go down on your wrath, nor give place to the devil. Let him who stole steal no longer, but rather let him labor, working with his hands what is good, that he may have something to give him who has need. Let no corrupt word proceed out of your mouth, but what is good for necessary edification, that it may impart grace to the hearers. And do not grieve the Holy Spirit of God, by whom you were sealed for the day of redemption. Let all bitterness, wrath, anger, clamor, and evil speaking be put away from you, with all malice. And be kind to one another, tenderhearted, forgiving one another, even as God in Christ forgave you.

This very clear and direct passage in Ephesians, like the passage in Colossians, also instructs us to "put off" the old nature and our former conduct or behavior. We are instructed to put on our new nature according to God in true righteousness and holiness. Verse 27 reminds us that when we conduct ourselves after our old nature, we are giving place or opportunity to the devil to move in our situation. Also, we are exhorted in verse 30 to be careful not to grieve the Holy Spirit by walking in the flesh.

Just from reading this passage, we see important reasons why we should be so careful to walk according to our Christlike character. In your own words, write some reasons you feel it is important to hold tightly to your coins of covenant.

_____

_____

_____

_____

_____

_____

_____

_____

_____

_____

Let's take another look in Colossians. It also gives us instruction on how to keep the new nature alive and strong. Let's read this passage together:

> Let the word of Christ dwell in you richly in all wisdom, teaching and admonishing one another in psalms and hymns and spiritual songs, singing with grace in your hearts to the Lord. And whatever you do in word or deed, do all in the name of the Lord Jesus, giving thanks to God the Father through Him (3:16-17).

This passage is a powerful reminder of the importance of the Word of God in the life of a believer. The Word must dwell richly in us. It must be our standard, our foundation, in all of our ways, our walk and our worship. We are to meditate on the Word, apply it in our own lives and teach and encourage others to do the same. We are to have a song of praise and grace in our hearts and on our lips at all times. And everything we do, in our actions and in our words, we are to do in His name, giving Him thanks and glory. If we truly filtered our actions through the instruction given in this passage of Scripture alone, what a difference it would make in us!

I want us to imagine if these verses were written from a "fleshly" perspective! If our old nature voiced an opinion, these verses might read something like this:

> Let the opinions of others and your own personal slant on situations around you dwell richly in you. Share your views, and instruct others to see it your way so that they will walk in agreement with your flesh nature, rallying others to join your cause, as they feel your frustration and justify you in your attitude. And whatever you do in word or deed, do all in the name of your cause and opinion, giving thanks to those around you who see it your way! (Unauthorized Sinful Nature Translation—completely unauthorized!)

Wow! You may say that this is harsh, but if we are honest, when we are in the heat of a battle, there are days we would rejoice to find those words in the Scripture. Our old nature tends to justify itself when it surfaces. But we must constantly remember our covenant with Christ. We are to put off the old nature and put on the new.

Let's look closely at the characteristics again that we are to demonstrate daily that are listed for us in Colossians: compassion, kindness, humility, meekness, longsuffering, forbearance, forgiveness, love, peace and gratitude.

Of the ten coins of covenant listed above, think about the list you made in your journal of the ones you feel you are more likely to "lose" when you are in a difficult situation. Remember that it is important that you are completely honest with yourself. We must be willing to acknowledge what we have lost in order to find it.

As our walk in Christ strengthens, these traits become more and more a part of our consistent nature and are displayed in us. The unbeliever may say that it is bondage or legalism to walk in this life with these characteristics as our new nature, but those who have experienced the freedom from the old nature would disagree. Walking in covenant, with the nature of Christ, brings freedom and satisfaction to the heart of the believer. When your old nature is dead you walk in true liberty. You are free from reacting to every negative situation or person you face. You allow the new nature to show forth and you have peace and walk in victory as a result. *And you become a real*

COINS, COVENANT & CHARACTER

nuisance to the devil! When he pushes your flesh button and you respond with your new nature instead of reacting in the flesh, you have won a real victory! You are allowing the characteristics of Christ to shine forth and your walk is a witness to believers and unbelievers alike. And you experience real peace, even in your battles!

It is a blessed life we have when we are walking in daily communion with Christ, with all of our covenant coins intact. You may be saying, "But what do I do now? I have considered the woman I know best. I have counted my coins of covenant, and I am missing some. How do I get back what I have lost?"

Let's read again our theme passage for this study:

I have considered the woman I know best.

Or suppose a woman has ten silver coins and loses one. Does she not light a lamp, sweep the house and search carefully until she finds it? And when she finds it, she calls her friends and neighbors together and says, "Rejoice with me; I have found my lost coin" (Luke 15:8-9 NIV 1984).

What did the woman in the Scripture passage do when she realized she had lost a coin? She became very proactive in finding it. She lit a lamp and swept the house. So, we will do the same and we will also find what we have lost.

Thy word is a lamp unto my feet, and a light unto my path (Ps. 119:105 KJV).

We will "light the lamp" of God's Word and His lamp will reveal truth to us! Once that truth is revealed through the Word, we will renew our purpose to walk according to the instruction it gives.

I seek you with all my heart; do not let me stray from your commands. I have hidden your word in my heart that I might not sin against you. Praise be to you, O Lord; teach me your decrees. With my lips I recount all the laws that come from your mouth. I rejoice in following your statutes as one rejoices in great riches. I meditate on your precepts and consider your ways. I delight in your decrees; I will not neglect your word (vv. 10-16 NIV).

> **Based on this passage of Scripture from Psalms, what are the important instructions given in these verses to us as believers?**

_____
_____
_____
_____
_____
_____
_____
_____
_____
_____
_____

_____

_____

_____

_____

Once more Jesus addressed the crowd. He said, I am the Light of the world. He who follows Me will not be walking in the dark, but will have the Light which is Life (John 8:12 AB).

Jesus is the living Word and the Light in my dark places. Through His glorious light, I will find what I have lost and will experience the joy of restoration!

COUNTING MY COINS

Week Three

POWER TRUTH

Week Three
POWER TRUTH
Light the Lamp

Thy Word is a lamp unto my feet, and a light unto my path (Ps. 119:105 KJV).

The Word of God will give clarity, correction, change, comfort and contentment. It will lead and guide us into all truth. When we miss the mark or stray from the path of our covenant, we must light the candle of the Word of God. We must put our trust in His guidance through the Word and acknowledge our need for His direction.

Trust in the Lord with all your heart, and lean not on your own understanding. In all your ways acknowledge Him, and He shall direct your paths (Prov. 3:5-6).

Allow the light of the Word of God to shine in your dark places, and walk in the light as it makes clear your path.

Week Three

Study: Light the Lamp

Week Three
LIGHT THE LAMP
Psalm 119:105

I have considered the woman. I have counted my coins. I have searched my heart and see the areas where I am lacking. Now what? How can I gain back what I have lost? How can I walk in complete covenant with Christ? Let's look once again at our theme passage:

> Or suppose a woman has ten silver coins and loses one. Does she not light a lamp, sweep the house and search carefully until she finds it? And when she finds it, she calls her friends and neighbors together and says, "Rejoice with me; I have found my lost coin" (Luke 15:8-9 NIV 1984).

Let's follow her example and do what she did. Let's light a lamp—the Lamp—and purpose to find what we have lost.

> Thy word is a lamp unto my feet, and a light unto my path (Ps. 119:105 KJV).

We must go over again the characteristics that we are to demonstrate daily as listed for us in Colossians: compassion, kindness, humility, meekness, longsuffering, forbearance, forgiveness, love, peace and gratitude. As you considered your own walk in our previous lessons, you are aware of how the Enemy comes against you to gain access to you through your old nature. While your weaknesses and mine may differ, the same Enemy seeks to steal, kill and destroy all that God has planned for us. And according to Ephesians 4:27, as we studied last week, the Enemy gains opportunity to do so by attempting to destroy our new nature in Christ. He wants to "resurrect" the old nature and cause us to walk out of covenant with Christ.

We know that the new nature and characteristics are desired by God in us, so let's look at the opposite of the characteristics of our new nature. The opposite of the attributes listed in our new nature would be characteristic of our old life prior to our salvation. So then the old nature demonstrates; lack of compassion and understanding; it is unkind and rude, proud, arrogant, self-serving, impatient, short-tempered and unforgiving. The old nature is not allowing weaknesses in others yet tolerating it in one's own life, not extending love to those deemed undeserving, always unsettled, restless and troubled in spirit, ungrateful, as a result of always seeing what they are lacking instead of the blessings of God.

When we break it down and really look at it, we don't desire any of the characteristics connected with our old nature to be a part of who we are. We know what the right thing to do is and understand the behavior that should be demonstrated through our lives as a believer. But knowing the right way of life and the accepted behavior is not usually why we miss

it—it is doing the right thing that sometimes creates the problem. We cannot just know the right thing to do and the Christlike nature we are to exemplify; we must walk it out in our daily lives. How many times have you heard yourself say, "It's easier said than done"?

God made it possible to live a life free from the bondage of our sinful nature! He has given us the assurance through His Word that we can live a victorious life and conquer the Enemy. He has made provision for us so that we can walk in covenant with Christ. The Word of God is our standard. Jesus is our sure foundation: "On Christ the Solid Rock I stand! All other ground is sinking sand!" Victory is available for every battle we face and restoration is assured for what we have lost through the eternal, unchanging Word of God.

> **God made it possible to live a life free from the bondage of our sinful nature!**

> *Light a lamp—the Lamp—the Word of God— and see those provisions!*

I travel a lot and I love it. But, anyone who knows me finds out quickly that I have no sense of direction. None! My sister, Judy, travels with me often. I love her company and we have so much fun, but unfortunately, she is as bad as I am (or maybe worse, if possible) when it comes to directions. I appreciate and am so thankful for modern technology—especially my GPS! I never, ever, go anywhere without it. Whether it is short trips, long trips, places I have been before or new destinations—my GPS always accompanies me. Judy and I have coined the phrase "directionally challenged" to describe ourselves when someone tries to give us a "quicker way" or "easier route" to somewhere. We always kindly reply, "Thank you for trying to help, but we have no choice but to go the way our GPS tells us!"

Our husbands are always uneasy when we leave for a trip without them because they know we will inevitably get lost if we do not pay close attention to where we are going, sometimes even with the advice of our GPS. And they are precisely right in their assumption! When I am lost, my GPS will give me *clarity* as to my location. Then it will reroute me as it *corrects* my wrong turn. However, my GPS cannot force me to go in the right direction. I must choose to submit to the correction given and *change* my course. When I do, I am then *comforted* in knowing I have turned around and am now headed to the right destination. What *contentment* is then mine as I am secure in knowing I am on the correct path! I can enjoy my journey while assured of my destination. Yes, my GPS is my friend!

As we have looked together at the characteristics of our covenant with God, perhaps you have realized that you have taken a wrong turn. Maybe you have been reacting in your situation instead of responding according to the Spirit of God. Now, you feel the sorrow of what seems lost. You're in a place you

never thought you would be. You may even be feeling like you are in circumstances that are painful and permanent. You may be suffering the loss of a relationship with a family member or fellow believer that you feel can never be the same. You desire to see God "undo" or restore what you have lost in the battle. Maybe you are blaming yourself for what you are experiencing. Perhaps you have been hurt deeply and it hasn't been easy to walk in love and show compassion or humility.

Now, you are struggling with guilt because you feel as if you have added to the problem by allowing your old nature to come "alive" in times of battle. But, we can find what we have lost! Our coins of covenant can be restored. Our old nature can be once again "put off." You can get back on course as you light the lamp of the Word of God. Like my GPS, the Word of God will bring you five important things that will help you in the restoration of what the Enemy has caused you to lose. These things are clarity, correction, change, comfort and contentment. These are the "candles" we will light through the Word.

The Candle of Clarity

Clarity will bring us understanding and give us the ability to make the right decision. Wisdom and understanding are promised to us in the Word. I need the wisdom of God in all of my decisions, from the seemingly insignificant choices to the most important. I need His wisdom in times of peace and in times of trials. Seeking God's wisdom will help me to make choices according to my new nature and ones that never contradict my covenant with Christ.

> If any of you is deficient in wisdom, let him ask of the giving God [Who gives] to everyone liberally and ungrudgingly, without reproaching or faultfinding, and it will be given him (James 1:5 AB).

> Who is wise and understanding among you? Let him show by good conduct that his works are done in the meekness of wisdom. But if you have bitter envy and self-seeking in your hearts, do not boast and lie against the truth. This wisdom does not descend from above, but is earthly, sensual, demonic. For where envy and self-seeking exist, confusion and every evil thing are there. But the wisdom that is from above is first pure, then peaceable, gentle, willing to yield, full of mercy and good fruits, without partiality and without hypocrisy. Now the fruit of righteousness is sown in peace by those who make peace (3:13-18).

God knows the hard places you have been. He has seen your heartache and knows your grief. He is aware of the pressures that life has brought. He is ever mindful of the Enemy's plot against you, but He has a powerful plan for your life. He is reaching out to give you strength, wisdom, instruction and guidance.

Read James 1:5 again. Write a prayer thanking God for the promise of wisdom and guidance.

_____

_____

_____

_____

_____

_____

_____

_____

_____

Therefore everyone who hears these words of mine and puts them into practice is like a wise man who built his house on the rock. The rain came down, the streams rose, and the winds blew and beat against that house; yet it did not fall, because it had its foundation on the rock. But everyone who hears these words of mine and does not put them into practice is like a foolish man who built his house on sand. The rain came down, the streams rose, and the winds blew and beat against that house, and it fell with a great crash (Matt. 7:24-27 NIV).

When reading Matthew 7:24-27, why is it so important that you live your life based on the Word of God?

_____

_____

_____

_____

_____

_____

_____

_____

_____

_____

_____

Remember, wise choices in our daily walk will always incorporate our ten coins of covenant!

The Candle of Correction

The truth of the Word of God will give us the correction we need to get back on the right path in our covenant walk with God.

> Every Scripture is God-breathed (given by His inspiration) and profitable for instruction, for reproof and conviction of sin, for correction of error and discipline in obedience, [and] for training in righteousness (in holy living, in conformity to God's will in thought, purpose, and action), So that the man of God may be complete and proficient, well fitted and thoroughly equipped for every good work (2 Tim. 3:16-17 AB).

When you read 2 Timothy 3:16-17, what are some reasons and benefits listed that assure you that the Word should always take priority in your life? How do you feel the "training in righteousness" referred to in this passage could relate to our ten coins of covenant?

_____

_____

_____

_____

_____

_____

_____

_____

_____

_____

_____

I seek you with all my heart; do not let me stray from your commands. I have hidden your word in my heart that I might not sin against you. Praise be to you, O Lord; teach me your decrees. With my lips I recount all the laws that come from your mouth. I rejoice in following your statutes as one rejoices in great riches. I meditate on your precepts and consider your ways. I delight in your decrees; I will not neglect your word (Ps. 119:10-16 NIV).

> **Based on this passage of Scripture from Psalm 119, what are the important instructions given in these verses to us as believers?**

_____

_____

_____

_____

_____

_____

_____

_____

_____

_____

_____

_____

_____

The Candle of Change

Accepting correction from the Word will give us a changed heart and will reroute our direction when we have made a "wrong turn" in our daily walk with Christ. I must accept the correction to experience the transformation of change. Read these familiar passages that admonish us to allow our hearts and minds to be changed by our relationship and our covenant with Him.

> And do not be conformed to this world, but be transformed by the renewing of your mind, that you may prove what is that good and acceptable and perfect will of God (Rom. 12:2).

> As obedient children, do not conform to the evil desires you had when you lived in ignorance. But just as he who called you is holy, so be holy in all you do; for it is written: "Be holy, because I am holy" (1 Pet. 1:14-16 NIV).

> To those who through the righteousness of our

God and Savior Jesus Christ have received a faith as precious as ours: Grace and peace be yours in abundance through the knowledge of God and of Jesus our Lord. His divine power has given us everything we need for a godly life through our knowledge of him who called us by his own glory and goodness. Through these he has given us his very great and precious promises, so that through them you may participate in the divine nature, having escaped the corruption in the world caused by evil desires (2 Pet. 1:1-4 NIV).

> *Write a prayer of commitment to God as you renew your desire to walk in daily communion with Him, not conforming to the world, but unto righteousness.*

_____
_____
_____
_____
_____
_____
_____
_____
_____
_____
_____

The Candle of Comfort

The Word will always remind us that we are not alone in our battles! We do not have to walk in our own strength. The Holy Spirit will comfort us and guide us. He will never leave us. He will teach us all things and bring to our remembrance the ways of righteousness. That same Comforter will bring peace and understanding, even while correcting and leading us back onto the right path.

> Jesus answered and said unto him, If a man love me, he will keep my words: and my Father will love him, and we will come unto him, and make our abode with him. He that loveth me not keepeth not my sayings: and the word which ye hear is not mine, but the Father's which sent me. These things have I spoken unto you, being yet present with you. But the Comforter, which is the Holy Ghost, whom the Father will send in my name, he shall teach you all things, and bring all things to your remembrance, whatsoever I have said unto you. Peace I leave with you, my peace I give unto you: not as the world giveth, give I unto you. Let not your heart be troubled, neither let it be afraid (John 14:23-27 KJV).

What is it about this passage that brings you comfort?

_____

_____

_____

_____

_____

_____

_____

When reading this passage, it is clear that Jesus was reminding us of the importance of keeping our commitment to His Word. At the same time, He was comforting us with the assurance of the promise of the Holy Spirit. The Holy Spirit will lead, guide and direct our paths! And the promise of peace is the result. We don't have to be afraid or troubled and live with the fear of failing in our covenant. The promised Comforter is here and He will lead us and never forsake us!

Jesus assured us that the Comforter would come and would lead us into all truth so that we could live a victorious life. The Holy Spirit will bring restoration! All that we have lost can be recovered and we can abide in the peace that Jesus gives in the process. Our troubled heart can rest by the still waters and our soul can be healed and restored as the gentle Shepherd guides us.

The Candle of Contentment

The Word of God reminds us that godliness with contentment is great gain. To have the characteristics of godliness that we have discussed throughout this study comes with great benefits in this life and in the life to come. When you walk assured of your relationship and in covenant with God, contentment becomes more and more a very real part of your life.

> Now godliness with contentment is great gain (1 Tim. 6:6).

> Not that I am implying that I was in any personal want, for I have learned how to be

content (satisfied to the point where I am not disturbed or disquieted) in whatever state I am. I know how to be abased and live humbly in straitened circumstances, and I know also how to enjoy plenty and live in abundance. I have learned in any and all circumstances the secret of facing every situation, whether well-fed or going hungry, having a sufficiency and enough to spare or going without and being in want. I have strength for all things in Christ Who empowers me [I am ready for anything and equal to anything through Him Who infuses inner strength into me; I am self-sufficient in Christ's sufficiency] (Phil. 4:11-13 AB).

In this familiar passage, Paul is saying to us that he has learned of the things that really matter in this life. His strength came from his relationship and covenant with Christ. He was empowered and ready for any challenge because of the sufficiency of Jesus Christ in him. This passage reminds us that we don't have to give in to our fleshly tendencies and pick up the old nature when we are in a hard place. We can overcome whatever challenges we are faced with, and that brings real and genuine contentment.

> We can overcome whatever challenges we are faced with . . .

Let your conduct be without covetousness; be content with such things as you have. For He Himself has said, "I will never leave you nor forsake you." So we may boldly say: "The Lord is my helper; I will not fear. What can man do to me?" (Heb. 13:5-6).

He has promised that He will never leave you nor forsake you. He is your Helper. He will be with you and you will recover what you have lost. Rest in contentment, assured that the battle to recover is already won.

> *Write a prayer of praise from your heart thanking God because He has promised that He will never leave you.*
> *He is your Helper.*
> *You have nothing to fear.*
> *List the coins of covenant that you intend to find.*
> *Restoration is coming.*
> *And so is contentment.*

_____

_____

_____

_____

_____

_____

_____

_____

_____

I will allow the light of the Word of God to shine in my dark place. I will receive the Truth and it will set me free. I will walk in the light that clearly shines on my path as I purpose to keep the Word of God as the Lamp in my life.

> ***When we miss the mark or stray from the path, we must light the candle of the Word of God.***

> ***We must put our trust in His guidance and acknowledge our need for His direction.***

> Trust in the Lord with all your heart, and lean not on your own understanding; in all your ways acknowledge Him, and He shall direct your paths (Prov. 3:5-6).

The word *direct* used in this passage means to "make straight and right." God will straighten out our path and put us back on course when we receive His guidance and correction.

When I am lost, the Word will give me *clarity* as to my location. Then it will reroute me as it *corrects* my wrong turn. I have chosen to submit to the correction given and *change* my course. I am *comforted* in knowing I have turned around and am headed in the right direction. What *contentment* is now mine as I am secure in knowing I am on the correct path! I can enjoy my journey while assured of my destination. And I will walk in covenant with Christ, demonstrating the characteristics of my commitment. Yes, the Word of God is a lamp unto my feet and a light unto my path. And I will recover my lost coins of covenant as the Light shines clearly around me.

Remember, the path we walk in our daily walk as a committed disciple of Jesus Christ will always incorporate compassion, kindness, humility, meekness, longsuffering, forbearance, forgiveness, love, peace and gratitude.

We lit the lamp . . . now we must sweep the house!

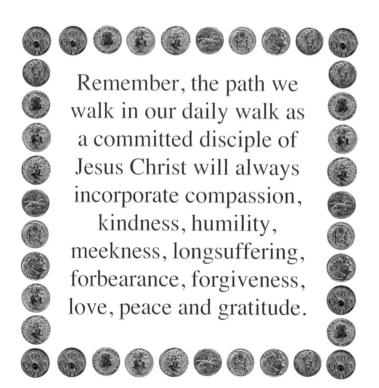

Remember, the path we walk in our daily walk as a committed disciple of Jesus Christ will always incorporate compassion, kindness, humility, meekness, longsuffering, forbearance, forgiveness, love, peace and gratitude.

Week Four

POWER TRUTH

Week Four
POWER TRUTH
Sweep the House

So repent (change your mind and purpose); turn around and return [to God], that your sins may be erased (blotted out, wiped clean), that times of refreshing (of recovering from the effects of heat, of reviving with fresh air) may come from the presence of the Lord (Acts 3:19 AB).

Repentance brings redemption, reconciliation, restoration and refreshing. Allow the Spirit of God to "sweep the house" by repenting of areas where your flesh nature has hidden the redemptive work of Christ in your life. Ask God to remove from you those things that are displeasing to Him and restore your Christlike nature as you draw near to Him with repentance in your heart. Sweep the house and find the lost coin!

Week Four

Study: Sweep the House

Week Four
SWEEP THE HOUSE
Galatians 5:24-25

Last week, we began by looking again at the theme passage of our study. We have been prayerfully searching our hearts in each lesson and asking God to help us gain back what we may have lost in our character. We have read that the woman who lost her coin purposefully took the initiative to "light a lamp" and "sweep the house." As we discussed in our previous lesson, the Word of God reminds us in Psalm 119:105 that it is a lamp for our feet and a light for our path. The Word is our lamp that will give us clarity, correction, change, comfort and contentment in our covenant walk with Christ. This week our focus will be to "sweep the house!"

The houses of the time this passage was recorded were simple and practical. Most of them were made with dirt or dust floors. It would have been easy to lose something as small as a coin in the heavy dust under foot. When she lit the lamp and swept the floor she found what was lost!

> **She found what had been there all along!**
> **It was buried under the dust!**

And the Lord God formed man of the dust of the ground, and breathed into his nostrils the

breath of life; and man became a living being
(Gen. 2:7).

With this passage in mind, it is easy to see that "sweeping the house" could represent getting the flesh out of the way. Our flesh was created from the dust of the ground and when we allow our fleshly nature to cover our Christlike character, we become less like Jesus in our daily walk. When we light the lamp of the Word, we can see clearly what we have lost. We must then go to the next step and allow the Spirit of God to sweep our house clean and reveal what we have had buried under the dust. The character of Christ will be found in us again.

Most of us have seen at least one episode of the many television crime series. The story will often begin at the scene of the crime. Yellow police tape marks the area and detectives are there busily attempting to gather evidence of the person responsible for perpetrating the act of violence. They look for DNA and any trace of a clue the criminal may have left. Then they use the evidence found at the scene to lead them to the individual involved. In these days of advanced technology, even the most careful of criminals are likely to leave something at the scene that is incriminating. Often, the crime committed was during an unexpected act of rage or fear. These crimes are referred to as "crimes of passion." It wasn't planned or premeditated. It happened as emotions surfaced and escalated! And when it was all over, the guilty person or persons ran from the scene, fearful of what they had just done, not wanting to face the consequences of their behavior.

> *Remember, this study is all about being honest with yourself so that you can find what you have lost!*

We know there are times in this spiritual warfare we are in that we find ourselves stressed and pressed, distracted and discouraged, frustrated and fearful, in our daily battles. We may find ourselves reacting instead of responding as God would have us to in the situations around us. We don't plan to be ungodly in our actions. No, it wasn't planned or premeditated! Everything seemed to catch you off guard and it all played out in a moment. Your flesh got the best of you. You lost—or maybe you willfully laid down—a coin of covenant.

> *When our flesh overrides our character, we always leave incriminating evidence at the scene of our conflict.*

We all have experienced times when we wish we could have a do-over—the times, like the criminal in the heat of the moment, when we react and our flesh nature causes hurt or pain. Maybe you were retaliating because you had been hurt by the person standing at the "crime scene" with you. You may have even felt somewhat justified by your actions because you felt it was done in self-defense. But the sweet Holy Spirit began to deal with you and remind you that you must display the character of Christ all the time, every time, especially in times of conflict.

Oh how we all wish for do-overs! I know I do. You may have heard yourself say these words: "I wish I could do that scene over again. I wish I had just stayed home that day! I should never have even answered the phone—after all, I do have caller ID. Yes, I knew better than to let myself get pulled into that conflict!"

> **_The devil will cause you to react and then overwhelm you with condemnation for doing so!_**

Or perhaps you have said this: "No, I am not going to just stand there and not say what I'm thinking! No, I am not the kind to just 'turn the other cheek'! That is the way I am and everybody who knows me understands my personality. That's just me and if they want to be my friend they will just all have to accept it!"

> **_This next statement is hard for us to acknowledge, but it is true. The devil will cause you to justify your actions and that is a doorway to self-righteousness._**

The result of allowing our flesh nature to surface causes either condemnation or self-righteousness, and sometimes both. These are hard to walk under and carry! And God desires to set us free from these heavy burdens.

You may be saying in your heart, "Oh great! I see myself in all of this. I have definitely left incriminating evidence at the crime scene. So what now? Do-overs are fantasies. I can't undo what I have done. My coins of character have been buried under my flesh. And now, I am going to run from the reality of how I behaved. I just don't want to face up to how I have been."

We may not have the opportunity to have a do-over, but we can have a spiritual make-over. We can prevent our coins from remaining buried under our flesh. We can walk victorious from this point on and we can rejoice as the gentle Shepherd repairs broken relationships and mends our own heart that has been wounded at the crime scene. Oh, yes, through a spiritual make-over—sweeping our house of the flesh—all things can become new again. The Lord can recover what has been taken as we purpose to walk in covenant with Him, allowing our new nature to be restored.

Remember the crime scene? The real criminal at the scene of spiritual battles and warfare is the devil! He is the source of all conflict and He desires to take our Christlike character from us and cause us to be defeated and discouraged. He wants us to react in the flesh and not respond in the Spirit. He pushes our "flesh buttons" because he wants us to leave incriminating evidence all along our journey. The devil hates character in the life of a believer. Why? Because it is evidence—real evidence of your covenant and commitment. It is evidence that validates your spiritual DNA. Christlike character displayed in your daily walk, in your good times of health, happiness and harmony, is evidence of His presence in your life. It is evidence of your covenant. Christlike character displayed in your season of sorrow, suffering and situations that you hadn't planned—is powerful evidence left at every scene of your life that points back to your new nature. It proves that a godly, committed Christian, dedicated to their covenant with Christ, was at the scene. And it is proof that you are not alone. It is evidence that the Spirit of God was present in your life in times of contentment and in times of conflict. It is evidence that His peace, His power and His provision were displayed. It demonstrates to the believer and non-believer alike that you have a real connection with the Lord.

The devil hates character because he cannot imitate it! He can imitate a lot of things and present a counterfeit instead of the real deal. He may attempt to imitate the anointing or worship and he may succeed for a season. He may attempt to imitate the character of Christ, but he fails every time. It is impossible for him to keep from reacting according to the flesh. He cannot mimic compassion, kindness, humility, meekness, longsuffering, forbearance, forgiveness, love, peace and gratitude. These represent the new and redeemed nature. And the redeemed nature is not in him and he hates it displayed in you.

You may say then, "What now? How do I sweep my house of my flesh nature? I love the Lord and I want to walk consistently in covenant with Him. I desire for His character to be reflected in me and through me. How can I walk in victory again when I feel I have been allowing my coins of covenant to be buried under the flesh? I want to leave evidence of my new nature at every place I walk. I want more than ever to be free of the old nature."

It is important to remember that it is not the intention of this study to bring condemnation. We discussed how condemnation is produced by the

Enemy. It always causes you to look at your failures and weaknesses and feel that it is impossible to change. Condemnation makes you look inward and causes you to feel insecure and inadequate. It makes the guilt heavier and creates a sense that you deserve what is wrong in your life. "After all, you are the one who failed!" screams the voice of condemnation.

But while condemnation *points at you*, conviction *points you to Him*! Conviction is from the Holy Spirit and draws you to the foot of the Cross. It pulls you away from your failures and turns your attention to the One who is able to forgive and bring restoration. Conviction connects you with the Savior. The Savior died to bring reconciliation and redemption to fallen mankind.

When we accepted the Lord's precious gift of salvation—became a follower and disciple of Christ—we put on that new nature. We entered into covenant with Him. This lesson is to remind us that when we fail, when we fall short, when we sin and miss the mark, we must be sure to acknowledge it and turn away from the Enemy's attempt to resurrect our old nature. We must sweep the house of our flesh. We must repent and receive the correction which produces restoration in our lives.

Repentance is characterized by a feeling of deep sorrow or contrition for our failures. But while you may be feeling deep sorrow for leaving incriminating evidence, the Word of God assures us of His faithfulness to forgive and restore!

My little children, these things I write to you, so that you may not sin. And if anyone sins, we have an Advocate with the Father, Jesus Christ the righteous. And He Himself is the propitiation for our sins, and not for ours only but also for the whole world (1 John 2:1-2).

An advocate is a person who pleads or speaks on behalf and for the benefit of the one they represent. Jesus is our Advocate and our Mediator, interceding and speaking on our behalf!

For there [is only] one God, and [only] one Mediator between God and men, the Man Christ Jesus (1 Tim. 2:5 AB).

For Christ (the Messiah) has not entered into a sanctuary made with [human] hands, only a copy and pattern and type of the true one, but [He has entered] into heaven itself, now to appear in the [very] presence of God on our behalf (Heb. 9:24 AB).

Write a prayer of praise offering thanks from your heart that Jesus is our Advocate!

_____
_____
_____
_____
_____
_____
_____
_____
_____

If we confess our sins, he is faithful and just and will forgive us our sins and purify us from all unrighteousness (1 John 1:9 NIV).

> *What assurance is given to us in this scripture concerning God's faithfulness to us?*

_____

_____

_____

_____

_____

_____

Like the woman who lost her coin, you will find what you lost when you sweep the house. And when you have repented and are refreshed in His presence, you will feel the new redeemed nature once again. And you will realize it has been there all along.

> *From your heart, write a sincere prayer of repentance, asking God to sweep your house of the flesh and allow the character of Christ to be evident in your life every day.*
> *And then rejoice because of His faithfulness to forgive and bring restoration!*

_____

_____

_____

_____

_____

_____

_____

_____

_____

_____

_____

_____

_____

_____

_____

_____

_____

_____

_____

_____

Repentance brings redemption, reconciliation, restoration and refreshing in His presence!

Read these passages and rejoice:

In Him we have redemption (deliverance and salvation) through His blood, the remission (forgiveness) of our offenses (shortcomings and trespasses), in accordance with the riches and the generosity of His gracious favor (Eph. 1:7 AB).

For if while we were enemies we were reconciled to God through the death of His Son, it is much more [certain], now that we are reconciled, that we shall be saved (daily delivered from sin's dominion) through His

[resurrection] life. Not only so, but we also rejoice and exultingly glory in God [in His love and perfection] through our Lord Jesus Christ, through Whom we have now received and enjoy [our] reconciliation (Rom. 5:10-11 AB).

It was God [personally present] in Christ, reconciling and restoring the world to favor with Himself, not counting up and holding against [men] their trespasses [but cancelling them], and committing to us the message of reconciliation (of the restoration to favor) (2 Cor. 5:19 AB).

So repent (change your mind and purpose); turn around and return [to God], that your sins may be erased (blotted out, wiped clean), that times of refreshing (of recovering from the effects of heat, of reviving with fresh air) may come from the presence of the Lord (Acts 3:19 AB).

Perhaps, as you look back over recent events you have found that the paths that you have walked have led you to a valley experience. Maybe you have suffered because you have lost some coins of covenant. Perhaps you have grieved because someone else in your life has brought you heartache. Regardless of the reasons for your wounds, you need healing. You have truly experienced the pain of warfare.

You have searched your heart and have looked in the Word for direction. You have taken seriously the correction you have received from God during this study. You have allowed the light of the Word to shine on your path. You have allowed the Spirit of God to sweep your house. You have repented and feel refreshed.

> *But there is still hurt, still residue of the evidence of the battles you have faced in your life.*

"How will I survive this time in the valley? Will I suffer indefinitely from the results of wrong choices? Will I ever get out of this dark place?" Perhaps, you feel you have had spiritual surgery and you're hurting, needing to heal. Or possibly you have suffered because of circumstances that came at you quickly and unexpectedly. You have tried to walk in covenant and in consistency, but you are weary from the turn of events in your world. You want to walk displaying the character of Christ, but you are so emotionally drained.

In next week's lesson, we will talk about the recovery time and the faithfulness of Jesus during your healing process. Regardless of the reasons you are hurting, healing is coming.

Complete restoration of all you have lost is assured.

In your study time in preparation for next week, read the familiar passage of comfort that we all know and love. Read Psalm 23. Read it carefully and let it settle in your heart. And next week we will take a journey to "The Recovery Room."

Complete
restoration of all
you have lost is
assured.

Week Five

POWER TRUTH

Week Five
POWER TRUTH
The Recovery Room

Recover is a word we all like. It has a twofold meaning. It means that we "obtain again something that has been lost." It also means "to return something to a normal condition after it has suffered damage or injury."

Our hurts and losses that may have brought us to the Recovery Room are as diverse as we are. Though our pain may be from different circumstances, we are all here for one reason: we are here for our healing — healing that brings restoration.

The Recovery Room is a place of transition — a temporary place where the healing process begins. Rest assured that the Great Physician will never leave you and healing is coming.

Read and meditate on our beloved Psalm 23. The gentle Shepherd is with you every step of the way in the recovery process, and though it may be a hard place, the end result of your time here will be worth it all.

> ***Restoration and recovery are promised.***

Week Five

Study: The Recovery Room

Week Five
THE RECOVERY ROOM
Psalm 23

Throughout our study, we have carefully considered our covenant with Christ. We have taken a sincere look at the nature we are to demonstrate and live out every day as a disciple and follower of Jesus. We have read and discussed Colossians 3 and listed the ten coins of covenant and purposed in our hearts to hold tightly to each one. We have carefully evaluated the characteristics we tend to lose and have determined that we will guard them closely. We have been reminded that we are to be completely honest with ourselves so that we can recover what we have lost. We have repented for the times we have left incriminating evidence at the various scenes in our lives. And we have prayed that we would recover all that we have lost or even what we may have surrendered to the Enemy as a result of the battles we have faced in our Christian walk.

This lesson brings us to the Recovery Room.

Recover is a word we all like. It has a twofold meaning. It means that we "obtain again something that has been lost." And it also means "to return something to a normal condition after it has suffered damage or injury." When it is returned to its former condition, it is said to be recovered.

When someone has a surgical procedure, it is often followed up with a visit to the Recovery Room. The Recovery Room is a special place in the hospital that is equipped for the care and observation of patients immediately following surgery. *It is where the healing process begins. And it is a temporary place—a place of transition.* And visitors are not allowed in the Recovery Room.

As I planned the material for this study, I really wasn't expecting this week's lesson to be at all as it has turned out. But God had a purpose and I literally have wept in preparing this for you. I have instructed you to be honest all throughout our study, so I feel as I write this, that I am to be honest with you. *I am in the Recovery Room.* Yes, right this moment, on a Sunday evening after coming home from a wonderful church service, I find myself in need of this lesson. We are all in the Recovery Room from time to time as we walk with the Lord. We arrive here for different reasons and in different seasons, but it is always ultimately for our good that we are here.

Restoration and recovery are promised, but perhaps the greatest privilege we will have from our trip to the Recovery Room is that we will have the opportunity for some very personal time with our Great Physician. You see, in our spiritual Recovery Room, in this season in our valley, He never leaves us unattended.

Restoration and Recovery are promised . . .

He is the one who offers care and He is the one paying close attention and observing you while you recover.

Don't you just hate to go to the doctor? You make an appointment for your routine checkup and you plan to get there on time. But, it seems inevitable that you always get caught in traffic or take that "one more call" at the office before leaving for your scheduled appointment, and then you are rushed to make it. Or maybe you are going to the doctor because you are sick and need treatment. You feel so badly that you would rather cancel and stay in bed than make the trip to the office, but you make yourself get up and get dressed and rush around so that you won't be late. You frantically get to the doctor's office with only a couple minutes to spare and the parking lot is full. You circle and eventually find a parking place. You run in and wait in line to sign your name on the sheet provided to let the office staff know you are there. Finally, you can sit down and breathe. You made it just in time! And then you wait . . . and wait . . . and wait. An hour and a half later you find yourself still waiting to be called back for your appointment! The tired and hurried nurse comes to the waiting room door and calls your name. *Yes! It's my turn,* you are thinking. Then you go back to the second room—the room where you will eventually see your doctor only to wait some more!

Don't get me wrong, I really like our family physician. He is a great doctor and he takes quality time with you when you see him. And after all, would you want to go to a doctor who had no patients?

Imagine if you went in the lobby and all of the staff looked so excited to see you because no one else was there. Wouldn't that make you somewhat uneasy? Yes, quality care from a good physician and trained staff really is worth the wait. But it doesn't mean we like it. We are all in such a hurry and we have hectic schedules. Our time is valuable and we don't want to "waste it" waiting.

To make the time pass faster, I find myself reading everything in the room. I will read the magazines they kindly place there for us and I will read everything hanging on the wall. Often, the physician will place his or her credentials there for you. And I read them. I like knowing my doctor graduated from multiple universities and obtained high honors. Who wants a doctor who barely got by with average grades? Oh yes, I read them. I am glad to know my doctor is qualified with the necessary and impressive credentials, and I remind myself that he is quite worthy of the wait.

But I don't just want a physician with *credentials*. I want one who is *concerned*. I want to feel a *connection* with him on a personal level. I want to believe I am more than just a "number" and that he is accessible when I need him. I want him to know and understand my infirmities and hear him offer a valid *cure*.

> ***But what about our Great Physician?***
> ***Let's take some time here and look at His***
> ***amazing credentials!***

One of the first things you look for on your physician's credentials is his or her name. Let's look

THE RECOVERY ROOM

at the powerful name given to our Great Physician that identifies just who He is:

> For unto us a Child is born, unto us a Son is given; and the government will be upon His shoulder. And His name will be called Wonderful, Counselor, Mighty God, Everlasting Father, Prince of Peace (Isa. 9:6)

His name is Wonderful, Counselor, Mighty God, Everlasting Father and Prince of Peace! The Name of Jesus is so powerful—He is more than enough for whatever we face. The title "Wonderful" implies He is simply indescribable! "Counselor" means He is qualified to give sound advice. "Mighty God" reminds us that He is strong in battle and able to overcome any attack from the Enemy. "Everlasting Father" reminds us that He will take care of our every need and protect us from our greatest fears. "Prince of Peace" assures us that He can and will speak peace to our every storm and calm our hearts until it passes. Your Great Physician is certainly qualified to minister to your needs regardless of the circumstances that brought you to the Recovery Room.

> When evening came, they brought to Him many who were under the power of demons, and He drove out the spirits with a word and restored to health all who were sick. And thus He fulfilled what was spoken by the prophet Isaiah, He Himself took [in order to carry away] our weaknesses and infirmities and bore away our diseases (Matt. 8:16-17 AB).

> *This is amazing! With just a word He drove out spirits and restored health and strength to all who were sick!*

He personally bore our sins in His [own] body on the tree [as on an altar and offered Himself on it], that we might die (cease to exist) to sin and live to righteousness. By His wounds you have been healed (1 Pet. 2:24 AB).

> *He paid the ultimate price for our spiritual, physical and emotional healing!*

Jesus is our Great Physician. He is more than able and willing to heal and minister to us regardless of our need. And He is *concerned* for every need we have.

When Jesus heard what had happened, he withdrew by boat privately to a solitary place. Hearing of this, the crowds followed him on foot from the towns. When Jesus landed and saw a large crowd, he had compassion on them and healed their sick (Matt. 14:13-14 NIV).

> *Jesus put aside His own desire to be alone and find rest because He was moved with compassion for the sick.*

Surely He has borne our griefs and carried our sorrows; yet we esteemed Him stricken, smitten by God, and afflicted. But He was

wounded for our transgressions, He was
bruised for our iniquities; the chastisement
for our peace was upon Him, and by His
stripes we are healed (Isa. 53:4-5).

You see, at just the right time, when we were
still powerless, Christ died for the ungodly.
Very rarely will anyone die for a righteous
man, though for a good man someone might
possibly dare to die. But God demonstrates
his own love for us in this: While we were
still sinners, Christ died for us (Rom. 5:6-8
NIV).

These passages remind us of how amazing and
unconditional the love of Jesus is for us! He loved
us while we were still sinners and went willingly to
Calvary. He bore our grief and carried our sorrows.
He was wounded for our transgressions and bruised
for our sin. He purchased our peace through His
death and by His stripes we are healed!

*Take a moment and write a prayer of praise to
our Great Physician for His unfailing love.*

_____
_____
_____
_____
_____
_____
_____
_____

Our Physician feels our pain and understands our suffering. We have a very real *connection* to His heart because He knows us so well. He understands our sorrow and pain. And we always have access to Him.

> For You formed my inward parts; you covered me in my mother's womb. I will praise You, for I am fearfully and wonderfully made; marvelous are Your works, and that my soul knows very well. My frame was not hidden from You, when I was made in secret, and skillfully wrought in the lowest parts of the earth. Your eyes saw my substance, being yet unformed. And in Your book they all were written, the days fashioned for me, when as yet there were none of them. How precious also are Your thoughts to me, O God! How great is the sum of them! If I should count them, they would be more in number than the sand; when I awake, I am still with You (Ps. 139:13-18).

> For we have not an high priest which cannot be touched with the feeling of our infirmities; but was in all points tempted like as we are, yet without sin. Let us therefore come boldly unto the throne of grace, that we may obtain mercy, and find grace to help in time of need (Heb. 4:15-16 KJV).

Write down the comfort you experience after reading these passages of Scripture during your time in the Recovery Room.

_____
_____
_____
_____
_____
_____
_____
_____
_____
_____
_____

Jesus provided all we would need when He died on the cross. The cross is the cure for our sin, sickness and sorrow.

> Bless the Lord, O my soul; and all that is within me, bless His holy name! Bless the Lord, O my soul, and forget not all His benefits: who forgives all your iniquities, who heals all your diseases (Ps. 103:1-3).

> He heals the brokenhearted and binds up their wounds (147:3).

> The Spirit of the Lord is on me, because he has anointed me to proclaim good news to the poor. He has sent me to proclaim freedom for the prisoners and recovery of sight for the

blind, to set the oppressed free, to proclaim the year of the Lord's favor (Luke 4:18-19 NIV).

> ***Jesus is anointed to preach deliverance and recovery.***

> ***He will walk you through the process of restoration.***

Praise God for our Great Physician! Jesus' concern for us is genuine and He is always available to us. But remember the waiting room? We are not fond of waiting! Whether we are in the lobby of the doctor's office or in our spiritual Recovery Room, we don't like delays. "What do I do while I am waiting to recover? How long will it be until I am restored? How long until I have found what I have lost? And what do I do until I experience the healing of my wounds? What do I do in the meantime?"

The meantime is what I call "mean" time! In our spiritual life, the time waiting between the promise and the fulfillment of it can seem like forever. The time waiting in the Recovery Room until our restoration has come can seem endless. But I am convinced it will be worth the wait! The Lord has your best interest at heart. He didn't bring you this far to leave you. He will not begin a good work in you and fail to complete it.

> ***Restoration is what we will experience in the Recovery Room.***

Let's look first at the reasons we are here.

Perhaps, you feel you have had spiritual surgery and you are hurting, needing to heal. You have repented and the Great Physician has removed the harmful things that the Enemy planted in your heart, but the hurt of your personal failure is still so painful. You need to be healed from the lingering sting of condemnation that the Enemy tries to put back on you. Or perhaps you are recovering from a deep wound inflicted by someone who has hurt or betrayed you. Someone else stepped out of their covenant walk and as a result you have suffered.

Possibly you have known deep sorrow because of circumstances that came at you quickly and unexpectedly. You have tried to walk in covenant and in consistency, but you are weary from the turn of events in your world. You want to walk displaying the character of Christ, but you are so emotionally drained. You feel weak and are fearful of failing. Our hurts that brought us to the Recovery Room are as diverse as we are. Though our hurts may be from different circumstances—we are all here for one reason.

> *The reason we are here is for our healing—*
> *healing that brings restoration.*

Remember, the Recovery Room is a special place that is equipped for our care and observation to ensure that we will heal properly and our recovery is imminent. The greater the wound, the longer our stay will be here. Don't rush the process. Allow Jesus to mend your brokenness.

Jesus is our great and faithful Physician. He is the sweet Shepherd in the valley. When we are at our lowest point, He is there to lead us through. Sometimes we feel the frustrations of delay and the wait seems long in the depth of the valley. But while we are here, we can find rest in the green pastures and drink from the still waters. We are assured that He is restoring our soul, and we can find comfort in knowing that this pain is temporary. Yes, this too shall pass.

Our transition time in the Recovery Room can be lonely and you may feel isolated from friends and family. Remember, there are no visitors in the Recovery Room. Always be mindful that there are people waiting just outside, anxious to hear of your condition, praying for you and holding you up in faith to the Great Physician. Family and friends who have been in the Recovery Room relate to how you are feeling. Yes, fellow Christians, who understand your hurt and sorrow, even though you may not realize it, are praying on your behalf during your healing process and recovery time.

I think my sweet niece, Jennifer, must have discerned that her Aunt Rhonda was in the Recovery Room. She is very serious about her walk with God and she is a prayer warrior. She sent me a very encouraging e-mail that included this familiar and comforting passage of Scripture. In her e-mail, she reminded me of the faithfulness of our gentle Shepherd.

> The Lord is my shepherd; I shall not want.
> He makes me to lie down in green pastures;

THE RECOVERY ROOM

He leads me beside the still waters. He restores my soul; He leads me in the paths of righteousness for His name's sake. Yea, though I walk through the valley of the shadow of death, I will fear no evil; for You are with me; Your rod and Your staff, they comfort me. You prepare a table before me in the presence of my enemies; You anoint my head with oil; my cup runs over. Surely goodness and mercy shall follow me all the days of my life; and I will dwell in the house of the Lord forever (Ps. 23:1-6).

We're following our Guide, our Shepherd, our Great Physician, through the valley. Since we are following Him, this valley must be where He wants us to be for this period of time. We are passing through the valley. It is temporary. The Recovery Room is a place of transition! There is no guarantee about how big our valley is, or how long we will be passing through it. There is the promise, though, that we are just passing through and there will be a table prepared for us. His rod and staff will be there to protect and guide us along the way.

> *Don't settle in the valley. Don't plan on living in the Recovery Room!*

It is easy to get discouraged traveling through the valley. It is easy to forget what lies on the other side in the midst of the confusion and weariness, blinded by our tears of sorrow. It is a dark place, and it is easy to lose sight of our Guide as He is faithfully leading us through. The easy thing would be to give up, to quit following His lead, to settle and hide in the shadows.

It is a fact of life that we must all pass through valleys. But we will pass through. We will not stay there forever. And as we are in the passing, we can gain strength and comfort from our Great Shepherd—the one who loves you more than you can imagine. He is the one who has plans to give you a future and a hope and the one by whose stripes we are healed. He is also the one who has promised to never leave us or forsake us. He is the one who supplies all of our needs according to His riches and the one for whom nothing is impossible!

You may feel alone in this valley of recovery, but you are not. He is here. Nothing can separate you from His love. Read Romans 8. It is such a powerful passage. The chapter begins with *no condemnation* and ends with *no separation*! And right in the middle of the passage we are reminded that the sufferings we experience in this life are not worthy to be compared to the glory that will be revealed in us. Rejoice! You will recover all and your reward will be great in this life and in the life to come!

> Therefore, there is now no condemnation for those who are in Christ Jesus (v. 1 NIV).

> For I am convinced that neither death nor life, neither angels nor demons, neither the present nor the future, nor any powers, neither height nor depth, nor anything else in all creation,

will be able to separate us from the love of God that is in Christ Jesus our Lord (v. 38 NIV).

I consider that our present sufferings are not worth comparing with the glory that will be revealed in us (v. 18 NIV).

Take a moment and write some reasons that these verses bring you comfort and healing during your time of recovery.

_____

_____

_____

_____

_____

_____

_____

_____

_____

_____

He is watching over you with an eternal, everlasting love. His love will light your way and restoration will be yours. He is so close to you in the recovery process. He is pouring in the healing oil. You will recover. You will find all you have lost. You will heal from your wounds. There is no condemnation for your past failures! You will be rewarded for your suffering in this life, and nothing can separate you from the love of God!

> *Taking time to journal is very important during your time of recovery and restoration.*

> *It will bring you comfort and clarity.*

> *You will see your progress and it will hasten your healing process.*

When you leave the Recovery Room, you will find your compassion, kindness, humility, meekness, longsuffering, forbearance, forgiveness, love, peace and gratitude have increased because you have been so close to the Great Physician. You have had personal time with the gentle Shepherd of the valley, and He has brought complete restoration. Your commitment to walk in covenant with Him will be stronger than ever.

> *You will hear your heart say,*
> *"Rejoice with me; I have found my lost coin."*

Week Six

POWER TRUTH

Week Six
POWER TRUTH
Finders Keepers!

Praise God for the promise of recovery! We will keep our coins of covenant intact now that we have found what we have lost. Love solidifies our new nature; peace soothes us as we walk in covenant with Him; and gratitude seals all of our Christlike characteristics in our heart.

Purpose to allow His love, His peace, and a constant heart of gratitude to flourish in you and you will continually walk in your redeemed nature and in covenant with Christ.

Read again Colossians 3:14-15. Purpose in your heart to receive and apply the instruction given in these verses!

You will have a renewed and strengthened determination to keep what has been restored.

Week Six

Study: Finders Keepers!

Week Six
FINDERS KEEPERS!
Colossians 3:12-15

What a journey we have taken through this study together! We have purposed in our heart to hold tightly to our covenant and walk in daily commitment to Christ. We have rejoiced in finding our lost coins of covenant and now we will discuss how we will keep what has been recovered!

Let's look again at the passage in Colossians 3:

> Therefore, as the elect of God, holy and beloved, put on tender mercies, kindness, humility, meekness, longsuffering; bearing with one another, and forgiving one another, if anyone has a complaint against another; even as Christ forgave you, so you also must do. But above all these things put on love, which is the bond of perfection. And let the peace of God rule in your hearts, to which also you were called in one body; and be thankful (vv. 12-15).

At this point in our study, we know the ten coins of covenant well. The Lord has been so real to me in the past few months as I have gone over these characteristics and have prayed to always hold tightly to them. The Enemy is afraid of a believer who walks in total covenant with the Lord. Remember, he

cannot imitate character. And when we do not give him any place in our lives, we walk in our redeemed nature. Look again at the passage in Ephesians that we discussed earlier, paying close attention to verse 27:

> But you have not so learned Christ, if indeed you have heard Him and have been taught by Him, as the truth is in Jesus: that you put off, concerning your former conduct, the old man which grows corrupt according to the deceitful lusts, and be renewed in the spirit of your mind, and that you put on the new man which was created according to God, in true righteousness and holiness. Therefore, putting away lying, "Let each one of you speak truth with his neighbor," for we are members of one another. "Be angry, and do not sin": do not let the sun go down on your wrath, nor give place to the devil. Let him who stole steal no longer, but rather let him labor, working with his hands what is good, that he may have something to give him who has need. Let no corrupt word proceed out of your mouth, but what is good for necessary edification, that it may impart grace to the hearers. And do not grieve the Holy Spirit of God, by whom you were sealed for the day of redemption. Let all bitterness, wrath, anger, clamor, and evil speaking be put away from you, with all malice. And be kind to one another, tenderhearted, forgiving one another, even as God in Christ forgave you (4:20-32).

As we discussed in this study, the devil wants us to react in our old nature so that he can heap condemnation or self-righteousness on us, hiding our redeemed character. We have determined to stop that from happening anymore in our walk with Christ. We have spent time in repentance and in the recovery process. Now, we will discuss how we will keep forever what we have found again.

I remember vividly how this series of messages was birthed. I shared it with you in the Introduction of this Bible study. While standing before the group of ladies at that retreat, the Lord spoke to my heart three important points that will help us retain our coins of covenant. I want to share with you what I learned.

The first point is that *love solidifies* (unites and bonds) all the other ingredients of our new nature together. Love is the main ingredient in the recipe for our redeemed character. Without love, it is impossible to hold on to the other nine coins of covenant. Secondly, *peace soothes* the believer, making our new nature readily displayed in times of contentment and conflict. Thirdly, *gratitude seals* all the characteristics of our covenant tightly together because we focus on what is right in our lives rather than what is wrong, and this causes us to hold close to our heart the other character traits of our commitment.

Look at Colossians 3:14:

> But above all these things put on love, which
> is the bond of perfection.

Love is the bond that holds these characteristics together! When we have love, we have a powerful gift from God! Let's look at some wonderful promises concerning the power of love:

> Above all things have intense and unfailing love for one another, for love covers a multitude of sins [forgives and disregards the offenses of others] (1 Pet. 4:8 AB).

> Hatred stirs up contentions, but love covers all transgressions (Prov. 10:12 AB).

> Whoever would foster love covers over an offense, but whoever repeats the matter separates close friends (17:9 NIV).

> If I speak in the tongues of men or of angels, but do not have love, I am only a resounding gong or a clanging cymbal. If I have the gift of prophecy and can fathom all mysteries and all knowledge, and if I have a faith that can move mountains, but do not have love, I am nothing. If I give all I possess to the poor and give over my body to hardship that I may boast, but do not have love, I gain nothing. Love is patient, love is kind. It does not envy, it does not boast, it is not proud. It does not dishonor others, it is not self-seeking, it is not easily angered, it keeps no record of wrongs. Love does not delight in evil but rejoices with the truth. It always protects, always trusts, always hopes, always perseveres (1 Cor. 13:1-7 NIV).

When reading these passages, why do you feel that love is the characteristic that solidifies our new nature?

_____

_____

_____

_____

_____

_____

_____

_____

_____

_____

_____

_____

Yes, *love solidifies* the other characteristics. When we genuinely love others, it is so much easier to have our compassion, kindness, humility, meekness, longsuffering, forbearance, forgiveness, peace and gratitude intact. *Love is the characteristic that solidifies our new nature*!

"How do I hold on to my coins of covenant?" Ask God to give you a healthy level of His love for all you come in contact with. It will cause you to demonstrate the redeemed nature of Christ every time.

Now look at Colossians 3:15:

> And let the peace of God rule in your hearts,
> to which also you were called in one body;
> and be thankful.

This verse lists two important coins of covenant: peace and gratitude.

Let's take a look at the importance of peace. Always remember that *peace soothes*. We are instructed to let the peace of God rule in our hearts. "Rule" in verse 15 is the word from which our term for "umpire" is derived. Get a mental picture of this. When we experience salvation, the peace of God becomes the umpire in our heart, standing guard over our thoughts, declaring, "That thought is safe!" or "No, you're out!" or "Home run!" When we allow the peace of God to literally umpire our hearts, our thought process changes because we will not permit ungodly, discouraging thoughts to stay in our mind, destroying our new nature. Thoughts that derive from the old nature will not be permitted when we allow God's peace to umpire our thoughts. And that same umpire will allow good thoughts based on our new nature to flourish and enhance our Christlike nature. Peace is a sweet God-given comfort to us in a chaotic and uncertain world. So, *love solidifies* and *peace soothes* us in our covenant with Christ. Let the peace of God umpire every thought and *soothe you* in your time of trouble. The world cannot manufacture peace. True peace only comes from walking in covenant with our Savior. And when I have peace, and my mind is settled, my nature is calm and it is easier to maintain my redeemed walk.

> Peace I leave with you; My [own] peace I now give and bequeath to you. Not as the world gives do I give to you. Do not let your hearts be troubled, neither let them be afraid.

FINDERS KEEPERS!

[Stop allowing yourselves to be agitated and disturbed; and do not permit yourselves to be fearful and intimidated and cowardly and unsettled] (John 14:27 AB).

You will guard him and keep him in perfect and constant peace whose mind [both its inclination and its character] is stayed on You, because he commits himself to You, leans on You, and hopes confidently in You. So trust in the Lord (commit yourself to Him, lean on Him, hope confidently in Him) forever; for the Lord God is an everlasting Rock [the Rock of Ages] (Isa. 26:3-4 AB).

> *Explain why you feel it is important that the peace of God is demonstrated in your life before believers and unbelievers alike.*

_____
_____
_____
_____
_____
_____
_____
_____
_____

> *What are some of the rewards of holding tightly to your coin of peace?*

———————————————

———————————————

———————————————

———————————————

———————————————

———————————————

———————————————

———————————————

Peace is a valuable benefit for the believer. Real and lasting peace is a gift from God and belongs only to those who truly experience and walk consistently in a relationship with Christ. It is a characteristic that the world hungers for and it cannot be marketed or counterfeited. Cherish the gift of peace and share it with others by allowing your nature to be soothing to those around you. You will be blessed and so will those you know and love when you create an atmosphere of peace everywhere you go. Remember, leave your spiritual DNA as evidence of your redeemed nature and covenant at every scene of your life!

> Be anxious for nothing, but in everything by prayer and supplication, with thanksgiving, let your requests be made known to God; and the peace of God, which surpasses all understanding, will guard your hearts and minds through Christ Jesus (Phil. 4:6-7).

This verse shows us the power of both peace and gratitude. It begins by telling us not to worry, but to pray, and in prayer make your needs known and

offer thanksgiving. Thanksgiving at the time of your petition indicates that you believe in advance that your prayers will be answered. As a result, your peace increases. And that peace soothes your heart and is a testimony to others of your character.

Now, let's look at gratitude. We are instructed in Colossians 3:15 to "be thankful." The Lord spoke to my heart, saying, "*Gratitude seals.*" Yes, *gratitude seals all the other characteristics in our heart*! How? Because when I follow the instruction given and have an attitude of gratitude in my daily life, I am always looking for what is right in my situations and in my personal life rather than what is wrong. It is impossible to walk in gratitude while focusing on problems. And at the same time, it is impossible to focus on problems while counting your blessings. Gratitude will seal all the other coins of covenant in my heart. Because when I am thankful, it is easier to display compassion, kindness, humility, meekness, longsuffering, forbearance, forgiveness, love and peace because my heart is full of praise and thanksgiving. I am keeping my focus on Him. My joy increases and so does my strength to walk in this redeemed nature.

I will always remember a young mother at the retreat when I first shared this Bible study. She shared her testimony with me at the conclusion of a powerful service and time of prayer. She told me that she did not realize she had any problems "holding her coins of covenant" and could not understand why she seemed so unhappy. She said that as she began to "consider the woman she knew best," she came to the realization that she had lost her coin of gratitude. She shared that she constantly complained because she didn't like her job. She wanted a new house because now that she had two young children, this one was too small. She hated her old car but couldn't afford a new one. And she said the Lord began dealing with her to find her coin of gratitude during our time of prayer. Her whole outlook and demeanor seemed to change instantly! She said she was no longer going to complain about her job, her old car and her small house. Instead she was going to thank God that she had a job in this bad economy, that she had a home and a car to get around in, and most of all, she said that her focus would be that she was blessed with a family that loved her. I watched as her new nature came to light all because she purposed in her heart to be thankful. A thankful heart is a wonderful blessing and an attitude of gratitude is powerful!

> ***Take a few moments and write a prayer of gratitude focusing on your blessings.***

_____
_____
_____
_____
_____
_____
_____

So, how do we keep our coins? By making sure we embrace love, allowing peace to rule in our hearts and daily counting our blessings. This will cause us

to always have a heart filled with gratitude. Love, peace and gratitude are powerful characteristics that will enable you to walk in covenant with Christ every day.

Remember: *love solidifies, peace soothes, and gratitude seals* all of the other characteristics of our redeemed nature and keeps us from losing our coins of covenant.

We will not lose our coins!

No, we will rejoice and have a determination to keep what has been restored!

No more lost coins!

Finders keepers!

Conclusion

Coins, Covenant & Character

COINS, COVENANT & CHARACTER
Conclusion

Therefore, if anyone is in Christ, he is a new creation; old things have passed away; behold, all things have become new. Now all things are of God, who has reconciled us to Himself through Jesus Christ, and has given us the ministry of reconciliation, that is, that God was in Christ reconciling the world to Himself, not imputing their trespasses to them, and has committed to us the word of reconciliation. Now then, we are ambassadors for Christ, as though God were pleading through us: we implore you on Christ's behalf, be reconciled to God. For He made Him who knew no sin to be sin for us, that we might become the righteousness of God in Him (2 Cor. 5:17-21).

> ### *The old has gone . . . the new has come!*

Through Christ we have become the righteousness of God. Throughout *Coins, Covenant & Character*, we have purposed to walk in our new nature, holding tightly to the characteristics that please God in our daily lives. And as ambassadors of Christ, it is imperative that we display the redeemed nature as a testimony to the world around us. We cannot truly preach and teach reconciliation effectively without demonstrating the nature of Christ in our daily commitment. It is our character that sets us apart. Remember, the devil cannot imitate a redeemed nature!

I have been so blessed to have wonderful examples of those who have been truly redeemed in my life. I have witnessed the gentle spirit and tenderness of one who has served the Lord for many years. I have been mentored by those who learned and lived the power of walking in their redeemed nature. The end result was peace and they lived lives of contentment.

One of my favorite verses of Scripture is 1 Tim. 6:6:

> But godliness with contentment is great gain (KJV).

My mother was one such lady that exemplified this verse. She was truly content with her place in life. She never cared much for "stuff" (*well, except she really loved shoes!*) and she was happy simply because of her relationship with God and her family. She loved God with all of her heart. She loved my daddy dearly and he returned that love. She was a wonderful and loving mother to me and my sisters and a precious "Nonnie" to her grandchildren. She gently led by example and as a result, her family loves the God she served her entire life.

I want to be like my mother. She proved to me that walking in her new nature produced a life of contentment. She left this world for the next with so much contentment and confidence that she was

on her way to Heaven, that peace was so real it was almost tangible in the room when she passed from this life to the next.

You may say that you do not have that kind of heritage. *You can begin one now.* You can leave a legacy for your family and a testimony of your spiritual DNA—your new nature, your redeemed character—in the life of everyone you meet, especially those you love the most.

My pastor and friend of many years, Bishop Bruce C. Fox, has prayed this simple prayer for most of his life and instructs us to do the same by asking "that we always have compassion, humility and a teachable spirit" so that we will never walk away from our redeemed nature. He reminds his staff and the congregation that we must "be real" in our walk with God so that our nature reflects His. Compassion is a very real characteristic in Pastor Fox.

I want to leave a legacy for my children if the Lord tarries. I want them to know me now and remember me later as one who walked in covenant with her God, having compassion, humility and a teachable spirit. I want them to see godliness with contentment in me like I saw in my mother.

> *Through a life of covenant, contentment is produced, and you are blessed while being a blessing.*

Remember the "candles" we lit in lesson three of this study? One was the *candle of contentment*!

Having the characteristics of godliness that we have discussed throughout this study comes with great benefits in this life and in the life to come. When you walk assured of your relationship and in covenant with God, contentment becomes more and more a very real part of your life.

> *Walk in covenant, keeping your Christlike character alive, and like Paul you will understand true contentment!*

Not that I am implying that I was in any personal want, for I have learned how to be content (satisfied to the point where I am not disturbed or disquieted) in whatever state I am. I know how to be abased and live humbly in straitened circumstances, and I know also how to enjoy plenty and live in abundance. I have learned in any and all circumstances the secret of facing every situation, whether well-fed or going hungry, having a sufficiency and enough to spare or going without and being in want. I have strength for all things in Christ Who empowers me [I am ready for anything and equal to anything through Him Who infuses inner strength into me; I am self-sufficient in Christ's sufficiency] (Phil. 4:11-13 AB).

And when you fall short and miss the mark, or lose a coin, then once again light the lamp of the Word, allow the Holy Spirit to sweep your house and you will find once more what was there all along.

Yes, keep your *coins of covenant*!

CONCLUSION

What do they buy? *Contentment*!

And the person walking in covenant with Christ is blessed in both this life and for all eternity!

Let's conclude by determining to keep the candle of contentment burning in our hearts as we purpose to keep our *Coins, Covenant & Character* intact by walking in obedience to the Word of God!

> **"Rejoice with me; I have found my lost coin."**

Compassion (tender mercies)

Kindness

Humility

Meekness

Longsuffering

Forbearance (bearing with one another)

Forgiveness (forgiving one another)

Love

Peace

Gratitude (be thankful)

Additional Thoughts

This six-week Bible study by Rhonda K. Holland will bring new insight to Luke 15:8-9. We are charged to "consider the woman who lost the coin, for there is much there." As Rhonda brings to light the *Coins, Covenant & Character* of compassion, kindness, humility, meekness, longsuffering, forbearance, forgiveness, love, peace and gratitude, we are challenged to live a life with these "coins" intact by applying the Word of God in every area of our life.

Rhonda takes us on a spiritual journey through the following six-week study:

1. Consider the Woman

2. Counting My Coins

3. Light the Lamp

4. Sweep the House

5. The Recovery Room

6. Finders Keepers!

You will witness the healing power of the Great Physician in your own "personal" Recovery Room. He will enrich your life with contentment as He sheds light on your *coins of character* through His Word: compassion, kindness, humility, meekness, longsuffering, forbearance, forgiveness, love, peace and gratitude.

You will rejoice knowing that His love solidifies, His peace soothes, and your gratitude seals your *coins of character*!

Lorna U. Dosnell
Church of God
Women's Discipleship Coordinator

Other Products Available
from International Women's Discipleship

There is a teaching DVD that is available for *Coins, Covenant & Character*. The teaching DVD is designed to be used by a facilitator/leader in conjunction with the participant/leaders guide. The DVD can be paused for participant questions and discussion.

Feel Rhonda's heart and passion as she delivers the message of *Coins, Covenant & Character* in this six-week Bible study teaching DVD. Rhonda teaches on the importance of our ten coins of covenant that was birthed during a dream she received from the Lord. From Rhonda's dream, you will consider the woman in Luke 15:8-9; count your coins; light your lamp (God's Word); sweep your house; be restored in the recovery room, and find the coins of covenant that you have lost!

Teaching DVD, Coins, Covenant & Character
$59.99 (plus shipping and handling)
ISBN: 978-1-59684-676-0

PARTICIPANT/LEADERS STUDY GUIDE and
DVD COMBO *(for Facilitator/Leader)*
$69.99 Combo Set (plus shipping and handling)
ISBN: 978-1-59684-677-7

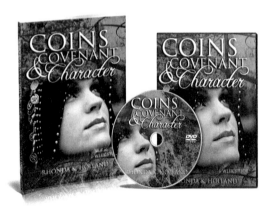

This teaching DVD and Participant/Leaders Study Guide & DVD combo along with the additional resources listed below are available through Pathway Press and Women's Discipleship.

Pathway Press
1.800.553.8506
www.pathwaybookstore.com

OR from Women's Discipleship
1.423.478.7170
www.womenofpowercog.org

Check out additional Bible study powerpoint resources available for download at:
www.womenofpowercog.org.

Check out our website for an Author's page with a personal blog from the author and submit personal testimonies on how these studies have effected your life: www.womenofpowercog.org.

Giants, Grapes and Grasshoppers is the first Bible study in the *Kindle the Power* discipleship series from International Women's Discipleship.

Author and speaker, Rhonda K. Holland, from Aiken, South Carolina, helps participants discover who they are in Christ as they pull down strongholds through the power of fruitfulness and praise!

There are two items availabe to purchase with this study: the participant/leaders guide and a teaching DVD taught by Rhonda.

Each participant will love having their own personal participants guide. Throughout the book are places to write personal thoughts and insights gleaned from the study.

PARTICIPANTS/LEADERS STUDY GUIDE

$14.95 (plus shipping and handling)
ISBN: 978-1-59684-624-1

Tier Pricing also Available (Price per Copy)
1-5	GG&G Participants Bible Study	$14.95
6-10	GG&G Participants Bible Study	$12.95
11-20	GG&G Participants Bible Study	$11.95
21+	GG&G Participants Bible Study	$10.95

GIANTS, GRAPES & GRASSHOPPERS DVD

Giants, Grapes & Grasshoppers teaching DVD is to be used by the facilitator/leader in conjunction with the participant/leaders guide. The DVD can be paused for participant questions and discussion.

A local church study group can choose to let Rhonda "teach" the entire lesson to participants or they can pick and choose what portions of the DVD to play during the study. The DVD is a valuable

resource. Rhonda is anointed as she delivers the taught Word. You will be blessed from her insight and personal testimonies.

TEACHING DVD

$59.99 (plus shipping and handling)
ISBN: 978-1-59684-625-8

PARTICIPANT/LEADERS STUDY GUIDE and DVD COMBO *(for Facilitator/Leader)*
$69.99 Combo Set (plus shipping and handling)
ISBN: 978-1-59684-628-9

KINDLE THE POWER JOURNAL

Kindle the Power Journal is a way to journal
your faith journey and personal testimony, detailing
answered prayers, and recording the "aha" moments
of insights gained in personal Bible study. Such a
legacy of meaningful moments can be passed on to
our children and grandchildren as a testimony of the
grace of God.

MY POWER JOURNAL
(for all participants)

**$12.95 (plus shipping
and handling)
ISBN: 978-1-59684-
626-5**

About the Author

Rhonda K. Holland is a women's conference and retreat speaker, minister and teacher of the Word. She and her husband, Kenneth, have been married for thirty years and reside in Aiken, South Carolina. Their sons and daughters-in-law, Joel and Lindsay and Jonathan and Emily, also reside in Aiken, South Carolina. Rhonda works full-time on staff

at the South Aiken Church of God where she and her family attend faithfully and are involved in various areas of ministry. Rhonda is known for "speaking an anointed Word in due season." She has a real passion and desire to minister to the body of Christ in these last days. Her heart for God and her love for the Word are felt as she ministers to those hurting and hungry for His presence.